Color Me Buddha

Color Me Buddha

EXPRESS YOURSELF TO DE-STRESS YOURSELF

Illustrated by Matthew Smith

BEYOND WORDS

Portland, Oregon

BEYOND WORDS

Beyond Words Publishing
1750 S.W. Skyline Blvd., Suite 20
Portland, Oregon 97221-2543
503-531-8700 / 503-531-8773 fax
www.beyondword.com

First Beyond Words trade paperback edition September 2016.

Beyond Words Publishing is an imprint of Simon & Schuster, Inc., and the Beyond Words logo is a registered trademark of Beyond Words Publishing, Inc.

For more information about special discounts for bulk purchases, please contact Beyond Words Special Sales at 503-531-8700 or specialsales@beyondword.com.

Manufactured in the United States of America

10 9 8 7 6 5 4 3 2

ISBN 978-1-58270-639-9

The corporate mission of Beyond Words Publishing, Inc.: *Inspire to Integrity*

Dedicated to my family.

(You know who you are.)

FOREWORD

I am inspired by everything I see around me. I take it all in: patterns, shapes, colors, nature, people... anything that catches my eye. I'm lucky to live in Hawaii, a place with incredible beauty at every turn—the emerald mountains, the azure sea, and the fiery sunsets that wash over the sky. They each influence my color palette as I create my artwork.

My subject matter is multicultural, which also reflects my surroundings. Hawaii is a melting pot of diverse backgrounds. I've been exposed to so many different cultures and environments throughout my travels around the globe. The themes of exotic or fantastic animals, East Asian–inspired costumes, and the spiritual variety throughout this book are an example of how this diversity comes through in the imagery of my art.

I am also motivated to create peace through my artwork. Peace starts with the individual. If I am able to make people stop and reflect on my art and lose themselves for even a moment, then I have accomplished my goal.

The Intersection of Spirit, Nature, and Humanity

Humans are basically students in the school of Earth. We are here to learn and to never stop learning throughout our lifetimes. Each person who passes through our lives or shows up to stay is here to teach us a lesson. Humans have the amazing capacity to experience so much through our senses and our brains. We are essentially the players in the game of life; nature is the playing field and the spirit is the playbook. The three elements of spirit, nature, and humanity are all intertwined and really are one and the same. Humans are here to live and love without judgment.

With this idea in mind, I approached this coloring book to pay homage to these three very specific themes that encompass our lives so completely.

Spirit

To me, the term *spirituality* refers to a higher power. Some feel this is one god, while other cultures have multiple deities. Whatever you believe, there is a common thread of a creator or creators—some type of divine overseer. I personally feel there is one higher power that every religion and dogma falls under: the Universe. The Universe contains everything and has all the answers. It manifests our thoughts, prayers, and requests, and it can be easily imprinted with our internal musings. Whatever thoughts we put out into the world will eventually appear in our lives. I am reminded of this whenever I draw an image inspired by spirituality. These drawings encourage me to see the correlation between my life and my thoughts and beliefs and to focus on positive thinking and actions.

Nature

A number of my drawings are focused around nature and the natural world. Nature centers us. It grounds us and gets us in touch with our place in this world. Spending time in nature allows us to reconnect with ourselves. When I float in the ocean or hike in the mountains, I feel at peace, in the moment, and in awe of the beauty that surrounds me. I let my stresses melt away and immerse myself in nature. My thoughts are still present, but the focus switches and I become the observer. The magnitude of the natural world is amazing; the number of plants, animals, landscapes, and wonders is simply staggering. From a larger universal perspective, our planet is a speck of dust. Nature is just one reminder of how small we really are. It is a wonderful tool we can use whenever we need to recharge our batteries and recalibrate the soul.

Humanity

There are two basic human responses to any thought, action, or experience: love and fear. Love is open and accepting. Fear is closed and dismissive. We operate best when we come from a place of love. Doing what brings us joy really allows us to experience life at its fullest. I love to create art; coloring my art is the most enjoyable part of my creation process. When we color, we experience the same joy we felt as children with our coloring books and crayons. It puts us in "love mode," and we can be so immersed in the experience and have so much fun that it becomes the most blissful escape. I want people to be able to tap into that childlike state of joy.

Through this medium we can all transcend age and circumstance, setting our inner child free and lightening our load one coloring page at a time.

Art as Meditation

Art—both creating it and viewing it—is meditative. When I start a new piece, I truly get lost in it. At the same time, I need to stay focused on the task of creating, which keeps me in the moment. The joy of creating and the gift of being present produce a beautiful dynamic that pauses the inner dialogue of my mind. Viewing a beautiful piece of art has the same effect on me; it calms my racing mind but keeps me grounded in the present moment as an observer. This is the goal of meditation: peace of mind.

Coloring books combine the two seemingly contradictory concepts of intense focus and relaxation to form a perfect meditation. A part of our mind is forced to remain in the moment as we put color to paper and concentrate on our digital dexterity, while another part can relax and let go of the day's stresses or tomorrow's to-do list. Eventually you can simply enjoy the act of following the lines on the page and filling the shapes with color. I hope this activity and attendant mindfulness bring you, the colorist, a sense of calm and peace.

The images in this book are rooted in my overall style and approach to art as a whole. The motifs of East meets West, the line work of Eastern art, and the imagery from Eastern spirituality and nature speak to me as an artist and as a person. I tried to convey these concepts from my own artistic perspective in an effort to create thought-provoking imagery that would be enjoyable to color. I endeavored to inspire an interaction between the art and the colorist. Essentially, these illustrations are half-finished. I started them by creating the foundation with the composition and line work, but the colorist is called upon to complete them. The beauty of this collaboration is that no two finished pieces are alike. Each piece will blend the colorist's personal aesthetic and color palette with the initial template to create a wonderful and unique work of art.

I hope that as you color, you will be mindful, inspired, and at peace.

Color Me Buddha

ACKNOWLEDGEMENTS

I am very honored to have this opportunity to express myself as an artist in this format. I would first like to thank Richard and Michele Cohn of Beyond Words Publishing for all their support. I would also like to thank Lindsay, Nevin, and the rest of the publishing team that helped get this project off the ground. Lastly, I can't thank my family enough for their support, patience, and understanding throughout the process. Thank you to my wife, Kris, and my sons, Sky and Jet, for your critiques and suggestions and for letting me take over the dining room table for months. To my parents, Gary and Andrea, thank you for bringing me into this world and for a lifetime of love and support.

ENJOY OTHER COLORING BOOKS FROM BEYOND WORDS PUBLISHING

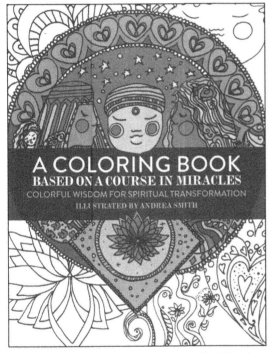

A Coloring Book Based on A Course In Miracles:
Colorful Wisdom for Spiritual Transformation
by Andrea Smith

Big Girls Little Coloring Book:
Healing Mandalas for Relaxation and Stress Relief
by Carol Omer

ABOUT THE ARTIST

Matthew Smith was born in Detroit, Michigan, in 1969, and moved to Hawaii in 1981. He graduated from the University of Hawaii in 1993 with a bachelor's degree in fine art and painting. Matthew has painted for as long as he can remember. His themes are varied, but the common thread throughout his work is a feeling of peace. Matthew paints inviting images he hopes will calm the racing mind. He says, "If my work can draw someone in and they can get lost in the piece and forget, even for an instant, then I have helped create a moment of peace. That is my aim."

PHOTOGRAPH BY JANET BECKER PHOTOGRAPHY